LaRie,
   Know that you are loved infinitely by God, and that He walks with you on your journey.

                    Peace,
                    Cindy Staton

Landscapes of a Sacred Journey

When the mountains, valleys and everything in between work together, it creates a beautiful landscape called Life.

Cindy Staton

Copyright © 2015 Cindy Staton.

All rights reserved. No part of this book may be used or reproduced by any means, graphic, electronic, or mechanical, including photocopying, recording, taping or by any information storage retrieval system without the written permission of the author except in the case of brief quotations embodied in critical articles and reviews.

Scripture taken from the Holy Bible, NEW INTERNATIONAL VERSION®. Copyright © 1973, 1978, 1984 by Biblica, Inc. All rights reserved worldwide. Used by permission. NEW INTERNATIONAL VERSION® and NIV® are registered trademarks of Biblica, Inc. Use of either trademark for the offering of goods or services requires the prior written consent of Biblica US, Inc.

WestBow Press books may be ordered through booksellers or by contacting:

WestBow Press
A Division of Thomas Nelson & Zondervan
1663 Liberty Drive
Bloomington, IN 47403
www.westbowpress.com
1 (866) 928-1240

Because of the dynamic nature of the Internet, any web addresses or links contained in this book may have changed since publication and may no longer be valid. The views expressed in this work are solely those of the author and do not necessarily reflect the views of the publisher, and the publisher hereby disclaims any responsibility for them.

Any people depicted in stock imagery provided by Thinkstock are models, and such images are being used for illustrative purposes only. Certain stock imagery © Thinkstock.

ISBN: 978-1-5127-2150-8 (sc)
ISBN: 978-1-5127-2149-2 (hc)
ISBN: 978-1-5127-2148-5 (e)

Library of Congress Control Number: 2015919465

Print information available on the last page.

WestBow Press rev. date: 11/30/2015

Begins with God

Ends with God

۴

We all have a <u>natural</u>
tendency toward what satisfies the flesh,
but I believe that we also have an <u>innate</u> desire
to seek true fulfillment, which is to
seek God.
The landscape of our journey begins with God,
and ends with God...How we choose to create
the rest is a journey from flesh to faith.
So let the journey begin.

۴

Many Roads to Choose

Landscapes of a Sacred Journey

Many Roads to Choose

Landscapes of a Sacred Journey

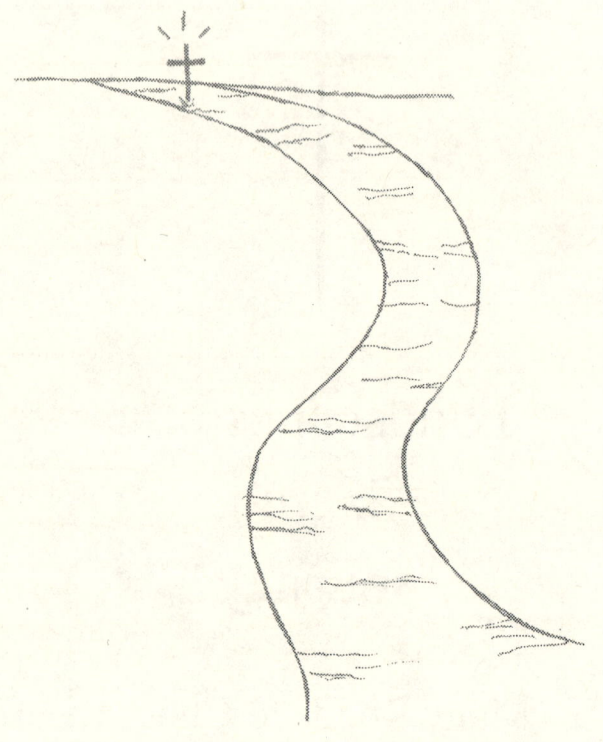

Landscapes of a Sacred Journey

ﻉ

Contents

Acknowledgements xv
Preface xvii

Part One

1. From Rebellion to Religion 3
   The Great Divide Between Flesh and Faith
2. Miracle after Miracle 9
3. Destination Denmark 15
4. Lord, You Want Me to Go to Prison? 23
5. Triumph to Tribulation 31
   A Fall from Grace

Wilderness Wandering 39

6. The Journey Home 41
   The Path that Led Me Home

Part Two

7. Babi 49
8. Be Still and Know that I Am God 61
9. The Can Man 69

Part Three

10. Meditations and Musings on Life, Death, and Letting Go 75
11. Strength in Weakness 77
12. IF 79
13. Rest in Me 81
14. Faith-filled Fog 83
15. Hands 85
16. Sacred Moments With Tree 87
17. Growth in the Silence 93
18. New Life 95
19. Release and Reshape 97
20. Let God Be God 99
21. Is There Death? 101
22. A Dead End 103
23. Legacies 105
Conclusion 107
Bibliography 111
My Personal Thanks 113

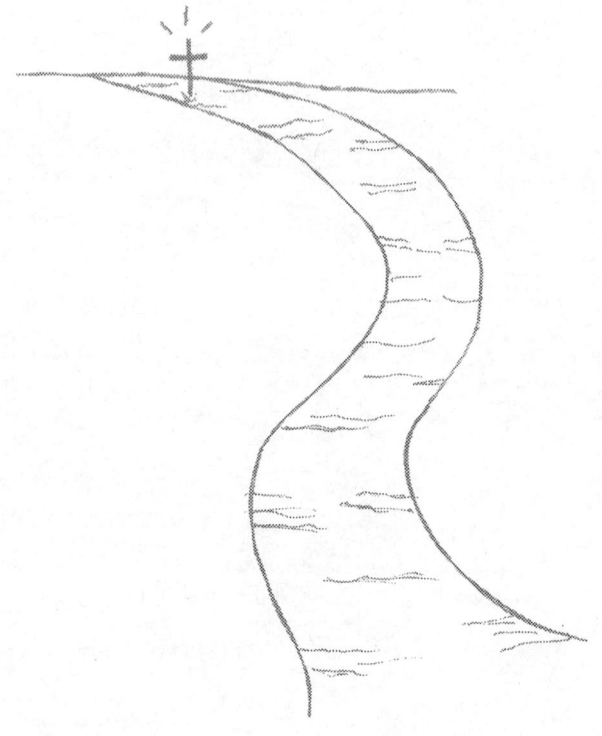

Landscapes of a Sacred Journey

۴

Acknowledgements

Writing this book has been a journey in and of itself. To relive all the stories and miracles has been both healing and exhilarating. It is with deep gratitude and humility that I share my journey of faith.

Words sometimes fall short of the depth of what I feel when reliving all that He has done and continues to do in and through me.

This book would not be a reality without God having placed many people on the path of my life prodding me and encouraging me along the way; trying to convince me that I have something worth sharing. To my family and many friends, and most importantly to the Lord I thank you.

This is His book and my prayer is that my life stories and musings about life will touch hearts.

May all those who read be open to receive and believe.

God Bless

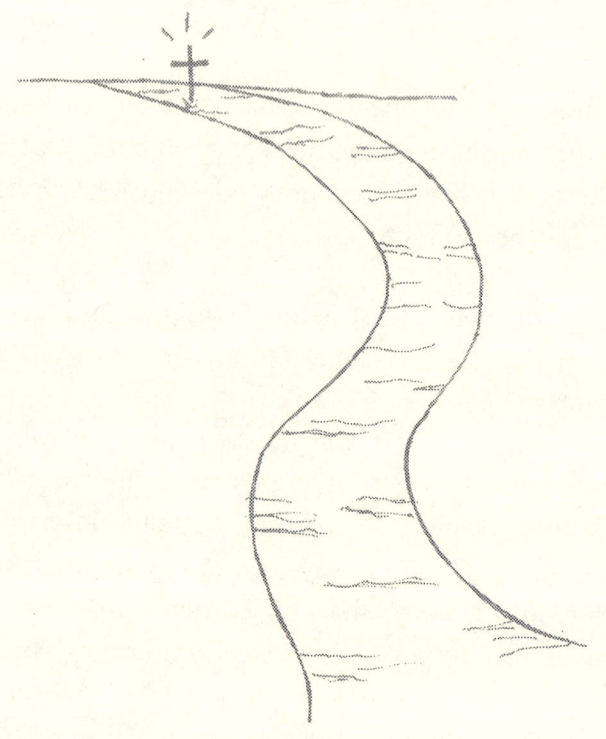

Landscapes of a Sacred Journey

Preface

As I prayed about how to write this book, I stood back and looked from a distance at my life. I wondered how I was going to blend it together into some sensible story. I heard the Lord say, "Paint the landscape of your life with words." As I continued to reflect, it made perfect sense. He showed me that a beautiful landscape is viewed from a distance. You're able to see how it all works together to become the masterpiece it is. My life and who I am today is because of all of it—the deep valleys, the mountaintops, and everything in between.

> In all things God works for the good of those who love Him, who have been called according to His purpose. (Romans 8:28)

Do I wish there were a lot less pitfalls along my path? Yes, but even those times of darkness and the choices I made that were not right for me are part of my landscape, and I met some wonderful people along the way who have been great blessings.

This book is a snapshot of the landscape of my life with its trials and triumphs—from deep valleys of depression, mixed with times of sexual promiscuity, and a lifelong battle with food addiction, to mountaintop miracles of grace. In spite of my inner struggles, God blessed me with many opportunities and many miracles I believe need to be shared.

Prior to my decision to write this book, I was introduced to Matthew Kelly's work. He is a Catholic evangelist and says, "God's dream for you is to become the best version of yourself, whatever that is." I had continued to struggle with my food addiction and eventually realized I would never fully realize the dream God has for me as long as food ran my life. Food was still my god. I was ready with the help of Gods grace to begin putting food in its rightful place in my life. I began eating healthfully and working out. With the help of a trainer, the support of a life coach, and the love and support of many others God placed in my life, I have lost 145 pounds. It is a daily decision. My weight loss journey has been and will continue to be a spiritual journey. The next step is to continue walking the walk and sharing my story with all those who care to listen.

As you read, may you become aware of your own struggles and the ways you have been held back from realizing God's dream for you. We all have a similar story. The characters are different, and the circumstances and weaknesses may be different, but we all have a landscape that we may wish looked different. But when the struggles lead us to a place of surrender, it is a gift. Know that no matter what you've done or where you've been, He can and will use you in spite of it; sometimes *because* of it.

We are all on the journey called life, wrestling, working it all out, and trying to find our way to our heavenly home. I believe there is an innate desire within each of us to seek fulfillment and love. However, we often choose the way of the world, which will never fully satisfy. The world has many idols that we turn to in an attempt to make us feel better. At best, they are distractions rather than satisfaction. Jesus said in the gospel of (John 14:6), "I Am the Way, the Truth, and the Life."

It is my prayer that as you read this book, you will look at the landscape of your own life and see that God has been there, He is there, and He will remain there. Yours can be a landscape of beauty because He uses all of it to blend together your masterpiece as well.

Part One

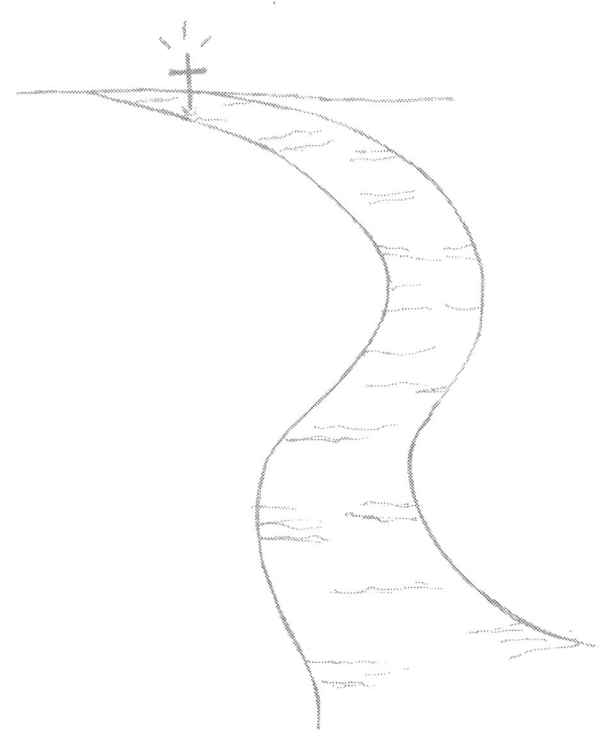

Landscapes of a Sacred Journey

The Great Divide Between Flesh and Faith

What side are you on?

Chapter 1

From Rebellion to Religion

The Great Divide Between Flesh and Faith

ﭪ

I grew up in the United Church of Christ. I really had no interest in God and was a Sunday school dropout at age seven. I drudged my way through confirmation. Got the picture? I did, however, sing in the choir with my father. He was the star in our church choir. That's where I got my natural singing ability.

My rebellion continued through most of junior high until I was facing a possible school suspension. That scared me. Fortunately, I was welcomed into a group of new friends who were good kids. My grades began to improve, and I was happy to get turned around.

To fast-forward a bit, I did pretty well in high school. I was in concert choir and participated in school musicals. I wasn't a star by any stretch, but that was okay. I never wanted to bring too much attention to myself.

After graduation, I got a factory job, working second shift. I also got drawn into the bar scene and all that can come from that atmosphere. I was drunk nearly every night. I experimented with drugs and ate my way to well over 250 pounds. While my addictive personality was in full swing, my addiction to food seemed to outweigh the alcohol and drugs. I remember going to a drive-in movie by myself and buying enough food for a carload and eating it all. There was a time when I drove from one side of town to the other, stopping at every convenience store, buying at least three candy bars at each, and eating them before getting to next store.

I gained twelve pounds in five days. Was it because I loved food? I was eating it, but what was eating me? It was a symptom. I was a fat kid, a fat adolescent, and a fat adult. Food was my friend—not! Food filled the void—not! Food numbed whatever I didn't want to feel—not! Food didn't love me, but it didn't reject me, either.

I remember the cruelest thing anybody ever said to me. A guy at the factory asked in front of everybody if both sides of me got wet when I took a shower. That shamed me into going on a diet and losing a hundred pounds. But did it fix anything? No. In fact, it caused me to become sexually promiscuous with men and women. It felt good to look good, and it felt good to be desired. But it didn't make me happy. The problem was inside; my lack of self-love. I remember wondering why I was ever born.

Out of guilt from all the wrongful relationships, I eventually began binge eating my way to an all-time high of 308 pounds.

My emotions hit rock bottom, and I wound up on the psych ward three times. I had two failed suicide attempts. I didn't really want to die; I just didn't want to feel anymore.

The reason I'm including this in my spiritual landscape story is that food addiction has been and will forever be a part of my life. It's part of my ongoing struggle that requires a daily surrender for God's grace. I know there are many others who also struggle with food addiction. After my stays on the psych ward and a lot of drugs that didn't help, I went to a weekend self-esteem retreat that helped me get a handle on things. I was able to look at what dwells beneath the surface. It was a beginning.

I eventually quit the factory job and went back to school. Hindsight is twenty-twenty. As I stand back and look at the continual rise and fall of my path, I can see clearly that I was always looking for that which fills the void. I know now that God is the only one who can satisfy the hole in my soul.

Is my story really much different from most? I don't think so. Going back to the days of Jesus, we read in Scripture of so many who were also in search of something. Of what? Of that which only God can fill. I am a Mary Magdalene and a prodigal. Aren't we all in varying degrees?

I thought I was getting my life together by getting married, but that ended after only six years. In that time frame, though, I met a friend who led me to a saving knowledge of the Lord. I began to read Scripture and sing.

One time a man came to our church to do a concert. He said, "There is someone here tonight whose life will forever change because of me being here." I knew in my heart it was me. I started building a repertoire of songs, and a friend of mine (Terri) and I began singing and doing concerts together.

۴

I was invited to attend a Christian Experience Weekend (CEW) by my ex-roommate. I went hesitantly, knowing I would be the only non-Catholic there. Someone there recognized me from a performance at a Christian gospel concert, and the cat was out of the bag. I was invited to sing on the weekend and then again at the closing ceremony. I had a powerful experience with the Lord that weekend. Never before had I felt such love, and I knew I wanted more.

A month later I was invited to a Life in the Spirit seminar at a different Catholic church. Once again I was singing with the group, and the woman standing next to me who's name is Lorrenne asked, "Where did you get that voice? You have the voice of an angel." I wasn't certain what to make of it, but I began to sense that God was doing something. As a result of all this, I became very curious about the Catholic faith and asked Lorrenne a ton of questions. During this time of questioning and searching, I remembered that years prior to this, I asked my mom if she would will me her mother's Bible. She decided to give it to me then. It was interesting that I was drawn to having that Bible when, at the time, I really didn't have much interest in God. I don't think I even opened it at the time, but something made me ask for it. God's prevenient grace was at work.

During my spiritual quest, I was led to take that Bible off the shelf and dust it off. I was thumbing through it when, much to my surprise, I found my grandmother's baptismal certificate. She was Catholic! I never knew it, as she had died when my mother was very young. Could it be that I was somehow drawn to the faith through her? A nun at the convent assured me that was very possible. This seemed to me to be yet another link in the chain of events that drew me to the Catholic Church. Lorrenne and I began to go to Mass together, and my curiosity became a longing. "As the deer pants for streams of water, so my soul pants for you O God. My soul thirsts for God, for the living God (Psalm 42:1–2). Nearly every time during the prayer of consecration at communion, tears would begin to flow out of me uncontrollably. Something so deep within me was happening that no words could describe. A deep longing to receive Jesus in Eucharist continued to build, but I was in turmoil about what to do. Do I leave my family? Do I leave the church I grew up in?

Lorrenne and I frequently visited the chapel at Sacred Heart Convent after Mass for quiet time. For three years I prayed, asking God to tell me what I was to do. Finally, He spoke to me while I was on my knees in the chapel. He said, and I will never forget this, "Your indecision has been a decision, and that's why you do not have peace."

The burden was immediately lifted. I jumped up and said, "I know what I'm supposed to do!" Lorrenne was my sponsor into the church, and that was the beginning of many miracles to come.

Miracle after Miracle

· Chapter 2·

Miracle after Miracle

۴

As a non-Catholic, I was never taught to put Mary in a place of honor. She was the mother of Jesus; end of story. I never thought much about what she must have gone through by saying yes. Her yes changed all of eternity. She is our heavenly mother. I once asked, "Why can we ask Mary to intercede for us?" The answer was rather simple and comparative. "Well, when you're a kid and want something real bad, most of the time you ask your mom, and she'll talk Dad into letting you have what you want." That made sense to me. So if Mary is our mother, she can intercede on our behalf to the Father.

۴

I began hearing about the apparitions of Mary in Medjugorje, Yugoslavia, and was given the grace to believe without question that she was and is appearing there, as well as earlier apparitions in Lourdes, France, and Fatima, Portugal.

I felt drawn to go to Medjugorje. I saved my money and got my passport, believing I was going. I didn't know when, but I planned to go.

The next year I learned of a trip scheduled for March and wanted to make the arrangements to go. However, when I had my income tax done, I found out I had to pay in, and it was the entire amount I had saved for my trip. I had no choice but to accept it, thinking that maybe I wasn't supposed to go.

One Friday night there was a knock at my door. I answered the door and greeted a good friend from church. I invited her in, and she handed me a stamped envelope. She said she was going to mail it, but at the last minute decided to hand deliver it. I opened it, and it was a friendship card, thanking me for being her friend, and so on, with a check for $2,000. The enclosed note said, "Have a good time in Yugoslavia." The miracle was that she didn't know I had to use my savings to pay my income tax. Nor did she have any idea there was a trip leaving for Medjugorje the following Monday. If she had put the card in the mail, I would have received it too late.

I called a friend who was going on the trip, and she quickly contacted Magi Travel. They were unsure if there was an available seat at this late date. She shared my story about the miracle of the money and said, "We believe there is a seat for her." They called back in twenty minutes, and all the arrangements were made. I left for Medjugorje on Monday.

My purpose for going was not to sing, or at least I didn't think it was. But through another miracle, I was asked to sing in the church of St. James during Mass. I sang "Surely the Presence of the Lord Is in This Place." I couldn't begin to guess how many thousands of people were there, and the altar was full of priests from all over the world. Someone came up to me after Mass and told me one of the priests wanted to see me. I couldn't imagine why. This priest was from Boston, but I don't remember his name. When he came up to me, he said, "I don't know if anyone has ever told you this, but you need to know your voice is anointed by God." He spoke with loving authority, as if he knew I needed to know this. I was so humbled that I nearly dropped to my knees.

۴

Being in Medjugorje was unlike anything I have ever experienced. It is an awe-filled holy place. I witnessed the miraculous phenomena of the sun pulsating and spinning in the sky, and my rosary turned gold. I had a powerful experience in reconciliation. I truly felt born again.

The humility of the people was moving. I will never forget watching an old Yugoslavian woman praying while walking on her knees all the way up the very long church aisle at St. James.

We climbed apparition hill, where Mary first appeared. To be among thousands of people in utter silence was miraculous in and of itself.

We prayed the stations of the cross while climbing Cross Mountain, the highest mountain in the area. In 1933, the parish of St. James erected a large, concrete cross to commemorate the 1,900th anniversary of Jesus's passion and death on the cross. During construction of the sixteen-ton cross, the parishioners carried up all the materials—cement, sand, water, tools, and so on—in memory of Christ's way of the cross. The cross was completed on March 15, 1934. It was a very rugged climb. It's hard to believe parishioners carried everything up that mountain to construct the cross. It, too, is nothing short of a miracle.

۴

On the way home, we all talked about our time and all the miracles that happened. The woman seated behind me on the plane leaned forward and asked if I was the woman who sang in the church. I said yes. She said, "I've been looking all over the village for you since you sang at Mass. I have to share with you what happened that day." She went on to tell me that her small group and their local priest from Ohio climbed Cross Mountain early that morning while praying the stations. They all remarked how they literally felt the presence of the Lord with them during their climb. When they came back down the mountain, they went directly to Mass when I sang "Surely the Presence." Every word in the song confirmed in their hearts that the Lord was indeed with them. What a blessing to be a part of that.

It turned out this woman was a travel agent. She called me a few days after I got home. She said Wayne Wiebold, a man who had dedicated his life to spreading the message of Medjugorje, was coming to speak at their parish. She asked if I would come and sing in conjunction with his appearance.

"Your whole trip has been paid for. Just say you'll come." So I was off to Columbus, Ohio, and sang in their parish.

۴

Not long after that, I received another phone call from Mary, the travel agent who handled our trip to Medjugorje. She said their local priest from Edina, Minnesota, had been on our trip and at the Mass where I sang. She said, "I can't tell you how strongly this priest feels about your music ministry. He wants to know if you would be willing to go back to Medjugorje with him and another group. Your whole trip has been paid for. Just say you'll go." So in August, I went back again and had the opportunity to sing on the top of Cross Mountain—a literal and spiritual mountaintop experience.

As I'm writing this, I'm reliving it. I have to sit back and take a breath. The miracles were happening one after another. For whatever reason, I was living in a grace-filled time, and it was very humbling. After all who am I that I would have all this happen to me, for me, and through me? I can only think that it was my yes to the Lord and a willingness to go wherever He led me that flung the doors of grace wide open.

I believe God eagerly waits for us to say yes as Mary did. She said yes, gave birth to Jesus, and gave Him to us. We must say yes, birth Him in our hearts, and give Him to everyone as well.

Copenhagen Denmark

·Chapter 3·

Destination Denmark

۴

I met a Presbyterian minister when I was involved in a Christian renewal movement called The Walk to Emmaus. His name was Oluf. He was originally from Denmark but was pastoring a church in Marengo, Iowa, when I met him.

I got a call from Oluf one day, asking if I would be interested in going to Denmark with him and a group of people. He told me, "I feel strongly about the ministry that God has given you through your music, and I want you to sing at the International Danish Church Days in Copenhagen, Denmark. I'll pay half of your way. Just say you'll come."

I mentioned earlier that I'd been doing concerts with my friend Terri. I told her about the invitation, and she was all on board to make the trip as well, so we were off to Denmark to sing.

When we arrived, Terri and I wanted to create as many opportunities as possible to sing. The sightseeing was wonderful, but our hearts were set on ministry. We sang at a nursing home/hospital-type place, and I will never forget it. I witnessed God move beyond the language barrier to touch their hearts through the music. Tears flowed when they couldn't understand a word of English.

There was another place, somewhat like a women's shelter, where we sang and talked about the Lord with the women who lived there. It was humbling to be used there and to share God's unconditional love with those desperate to be loved. I trust seeds were planted in the hearts and minds of those young women who were lost and broken.

۴

Then came our opportunity to sing at the International Danish Church Days. It was very exciting to be there and witness so many cultures and faith traditions, coming together in one huge event. Desmond Tutu was one of the main speakers.

We met a wonderfully spirit-filled priest at the conference as well. His name was Father Patrick Sheils. After hearing us sing, he invited us to sing at one of his weekend masses. So many blessings.

۴

One day Terri and I were having lunch at a Burger King in the northern tip of Denmark. I was never so happy to have a burger, fries, and a real Coke; a Dane I will never be. One of the women from our group sat down with us and began to talk to us about our music. "You need to make a recording."

We laughed at her and I said, "Yeah, right."

She was serious, so serious that she said, "I want to pay for you to make a recording." We were in shock, to say the least.

۴

We closed out our Denmark trip by worshipping together at a church where Oluf had arranged for us to attend. Terri and I sang there, as well. When we were about to leave, a spirit-filled woman walked up and handed me a piece of paper. She said, "I have a word of knowledge and prophecy from the Lord for you.

God has given me a word to you personally.

"You are My affianced, and I will go with you, and where I am, you will be because you will follow My signal and obey My voice. I have placed you to be a blessing, and you will bear fruit, and with your mercy it will be known on you that you are Mine. Give blessing to the smallest of Mine, and I will bless your soul, and you will radiate My love to your associates. Be free and thankful, for it is with My help you are set free. I love you so much, and you will reach to the highest tops of the mountains and be with Me in My kingdom. Go."

It was a message of love, a blessing, a commissioning, and a promise all rolled into one. I'm humbled every time I read it.

۴

Three days after I arrived home, I received a check in the mail for $12,000 from the woman who wanted us to record.

۴

The night I got home from Denmark, I received a call from my friend who had gone to Medjugorje with me. She said while I was in Denmark that she had heard about the Christian Artists' Conference in Estes Park, Colorado. She believed I was supposed to go. I told her I didn't have my suitcase unpacked and needed to take a breath. By this time, though, I'd learned not to question what God might be doing. I told her, "If I'm supposed to go, God will work it out."

Well He did. I was talking to a friend about the trip to Denmark and the phone call I received after I got home. She interrupted me, saying, "You've got it."

"Got what?"

She said, "I want to pay your way to Colorado." She wrote a check for $2,000. The generosity of people is miraculous. My head was spinning.

I went to the Christian Artists' Conference. I was one of the finalists in a competition and was able to meet world-famous Sandy Patti and Steve Green. I had the opportunity to talk to Sandi and tell her about the miracle of the $12,000 Terri and I received to record. Wanting to be a good steward of the money, I had no idea where to go to record. Sandi said—and I believe this is why I went to Colorado—we should go to "Pinebrook Studios in Alexandria, Indiana, where I have done a lot of my own recording." So off we went for an entire week of recording. It was an amazing experience that we will never forget.

These stories are amazing because we have an amazing God. I'm just an ordinary person. It is God who does the extraordinary in and through the lives of those who say yes. All He asks of us is to say, "Here I am, Lord, send me."

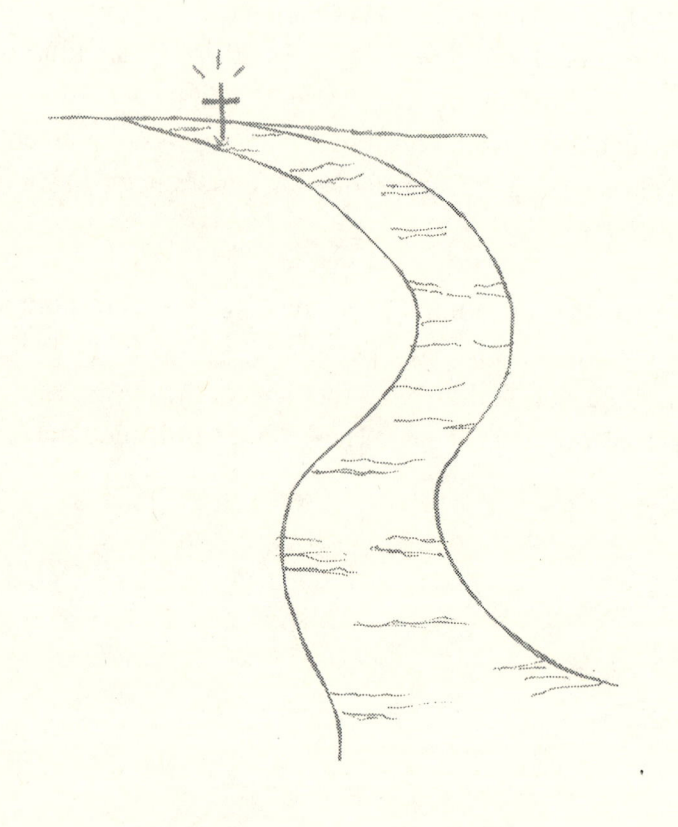

Landscapes of a Sacred Journey

There are many different kinds of prisons

Are you being held captive?

Chapter 4

Lord, You Want Me to Go to Prison?

A visionary from Conyers, Georgia, came to our local parish to speak of the apparitions of Mary. Her name was Nancy. I was asked to sing "Ave Maria" that evening.

Following her talk, Nancy came up to me and said she sensed the Blessed Mother was all around me. She asked if I would be willing to go to New Jersey with her and her spiritual director, Father Salazar, and sing in conjunction with her presentation. I felt honored to be asked and said, "Yes, I will go."

All the arrangements were made, but a few days before we were to leave, Nancy was in a car accident and was unable to go. So Father Salazar and I did the presentation. He and I had never met prior to the trip to New Jersey.

After the evening presentation, we talked about how we thought everything went in spite of Nancy's absence. In response to the music, he said, "Your voice is ethereal." I didn't know what that word meant at the time and was astounded to learn it means "heavenly" or "celestial."

۴

So often through the years, people have said, "You have the voice of an angel." I know that it comes from beyond me. It's God's presence and the open hearts of those who hear that make the difference. I'm merely the mouthpiece He's chosen. He's the one who reaches into the hearts and minds of those who are hungry to hear and experience His love.

۴

Father Salazar was a prison chaplain in Miami, Florida, and before we left New Jersey, he asked if I would come to Miami and do a concert for the inmates. Even though I didn't know how it would work, I said yes. When I got home, my church's spiritual growth committee went to work promoting a fund-raising concert to raise money for my trip to Florida.

Remember Lorrenne? Her sister lived in Florida, so Lorrenne and I made the trip together. Through other mutual acquaintances in Florida, arrangements were made for me to have a radio interview with Johnette Benkovic, the host of the well-known EWTN program *Women of Grace*. I was also able to do several other church concerts in the area.

Our next stop was the prison. Just before we arrived, I asked Lorrenne if she would talk to the inmates midway through the concert. I caught her off guard. Initially she thought, what in the world could a little old white-haired lady possibly say to these men. As she thought about it more, she knew she could talk to them as a mother who has sons. She thought about it more and asked, "Could it be that I could somehow stand in the gap and apologize to these men for any hurts that may have been caused by their own mothers?" From the heart of a mother to the wounded heart of a son.

On arriving at the prison, we had to go through many security checks to bring in my sound equipment. It was, to say the least, an eerie feeling every time we saw and heard the iron doors shut behind us. We weren't even allowed to go to the bathroom alone.

We finally made our way to the chapel and got set up. The inmates began to arrive, and Lorrenne and I prayed that God would touch their hearts. He gave us a real sense of compassion for these men. Though we knew they were serving time for crimes they committed, we were able to see beyond the crimes and know that underneath the behaviors were many wounded hearts.

It was a powerful and humbling experience to see how God touched the hardened hearts of these men. Many were moved to tears. After the concert, several came up and hugged us with tears of surrender and gratitude that we came. It was an honor to be there and witness God reaching into their hearts with a message of His unconditional love through music and a little, old, white-haired lady. God did the extraordinary through the ordinary, and I will never forget it.

۴

Leaving that experience made me think about all the ways we imprison ourselves. There are prisons within the walls of our hearts that are equally confining as those with bars. Life can be complex, and the ways we carry our woundedness creates emotional chains that hold us captive. We are prisoners to addictions, sexual immorality, crime, depression, low self-esteem, fear, unforgiveness, and so much more.

We walk through life wearing masks that suit every occasion so that no one knows how we really feel. If only we could see ourselves through the eyes of love that Jesus does.

۴

I invite you to take some time in the quiet of your own heart to get in touch with the ways you are being held captive. Has an event or relationship wounded you so that you just can't let it go? Is it an addiction that runs rampant in an effort to stay ahead of feeling too much? Too much pain? Too much fear? Too much loss? Too much anger? Too much loneliness? Too much of the unknown? Too much regret? Too much shame? Too much guilt? Think of how it might feel to be free of what binds and confines you. Does it feel good, or does it bring up a whole new set of fears? You see, there is security in misery because it's so familiar. The fear of change is yet another way we are held in solitary confinement.

Jesus is the healer. He longs for us to trust Him with it all day by day, hour by hour, and sometimes minute by minute. Let Him heal the shame that binds you. Let His love be the balm that soothes your aching soul. Let His love fill the void that no other earthly thing can fill. Be captivated by His love rather being held captive.

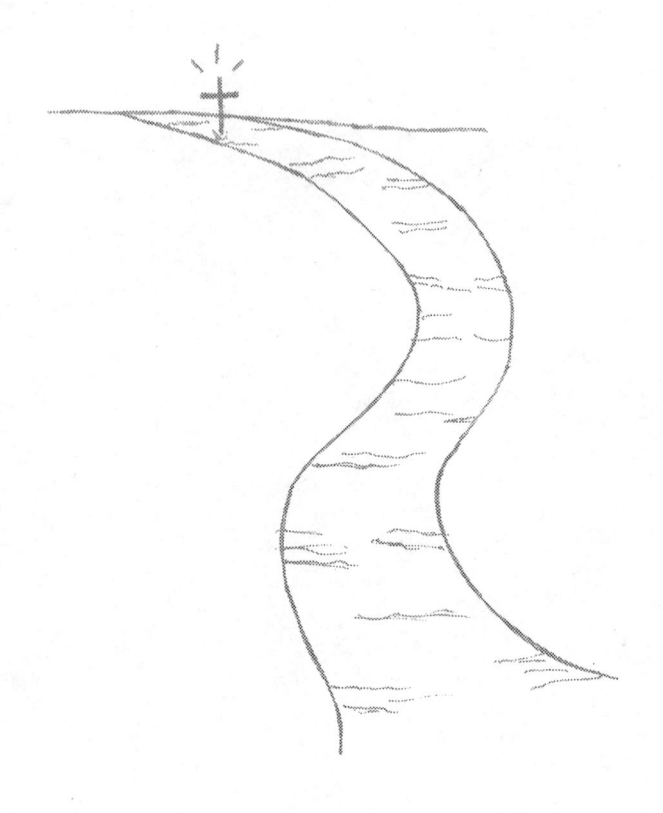

Landscapes of a Sacred Journey

Triumph to Tribulation

·Chapter 5·

Triumph to Tribulation

A Fall from Grace

٤

A path toward holiness is a long and winding road with many hills, valleys and falls. "for all have sinned and fall short of the glory of God."(Romans 3:23) Free will sometimes feels like a curse instead of a gift. Praise God we are redeemed in spite of our failings and short comings.

٤

As a new convert to Catholicism, my hunger for spiritual growth continued beyond the mass. I stumbled across a book written by John Michael Talbot. He, too, has quite a conversion story that I could easily identify with. He is a world-famous Catholic singer/songwriter.

He established a third-order Franciscan community called the Brothers and Sisters of Charity in Eureka Springs,

Arkansas. I was interested in finding out more about him and his community. He has a retreat center near his community. I wanted to go but didn't have a particular time or reason for going; I just knew I wanted to go sometime. I got a call from a friend whose mother was going to be driving to Arkansas and was happy to let me ride along and share gas expense. She would drop me off on the way to her destination and pick me up on the way back. The next day I received $300 cash in the mail from someone. There was no note or any way of identifying who it came from, but it was enough to cover my share of the trip. God takes care of every detail when He wants to get you somewhere.

۴

I need to share at this point why I had the freedom to travel during all these experiences. I owned and operated a custom sewn lettering business. Sporting goods stores contracted me to do the lettering on jackets, caps, and banners. People working for me covered for me while traveling. That may sound like I had a lot of money, but the reality is I did not. I barely kept the roof over my head, but I did have the freedom to go, and God obviously provided for my needs and worked through the generosity of many people to get me where He wanted me to go.

۴

We left on New Year's Day. I arrived to find there were no planned retreats. It was the dead of winter in Arkansas with ice in the mountains, which was rather unusual for them. Deacon Sam and a maintenance guy were at the retreat center, and a neighbor woman came for the daily communion service. It was an incredible time of silence and reflection, which was much needed and the reason I went—or so I thought.

One morning I went to the communion service, and after receiving Eucharist, I felt led to sing "Surely the Presence." Afterward, we went to breakfast, and Deacon Sam came to me and said, "John Michael needs to hear you."

"Wait a minute, that's not why I came here."

"I understand, but let me tell you, I see and hear a lot of people coming and going through this retreat center and there is something very special about your voice. You have an anointing, and John needs to hear you. He just got back from a world tour, and I'm going to call him."

I immediately went back to the chapel and prostrated myself on the altar, wondering what God was doing now. Yet I was able to say not my will but Thy will be done. God's orchestration and perfect timing of this trip was becoming clearer to me.

Deacon Sam came into the chapel and told me John wanted to meet me. The maintenance man took me in his pickup down a very scary, icy mountain. We arrived safely at John's community, and I went into the chapel and waited. I could not believe this was happening. To meet John Michael Talbot was, in the music world, like meeting the pope.

He walked in and greeted me. He asked me to sing for him. I sang what seems to be the song God put His thumbprint on, "Surely the Presence of the Lord Is in this Place."

Afterward, he asked if I was Catholic. I said yes. He asked if I was involved in the charismatic renewal. I said yes.

He said, "I don't want to sound crass, but you sound like a Catholic Sandi Patti." He asked if I would record a demo for him. Having no idea how that was going to happen, I said yes. He asked me to make a demo of just three songs and send it to him.

After I got home, difficult as this must be getting to believe, someone gave me $1,000 to do the demo. I recorded the demo and sent it to John Michael. I waited for several weeks and no word. Then one day I received a phone call from one of the sporting goods companies I worked with, offering me a full-time position as manager of their computerized embroidery department. I told him I would pray about it and get back with him.

I immediately called a friend and said I needed prayers for discernment. I said, "If I would just hear something from John Michael Talbot, it would somehow be a sign of the direction I should be going." I no more than got the words out of my mouth, and I got a beep coming in on the other line. It was John Michael Talbot. You could have knocked me over with a feather.

He apologized for taking so long to respond. He said, "This morning I just decided rather than to respond with a letter, I'd just pick up the phone and call you."

I said, "Let me tell you why you were led to call me right now." I shared with him about the job offer and my need for discernment and direction.

"I can't guarantee you a major label contract," he responded, "but I think I can make a difference for you. I'm going to write a letter of recommendation for you with the contact information of my producer at Sparrow Records." He told me to contact him and tell him of our conversation and the letter of recommendation.

I received the letter from John in a few days. I made several attempts to contact his producer but never made the connection.

At this point as exciting as this all was, I began to feel fearful of too much success. Was I ready for a possible major label and all that would be demanded of me?

It wasn't long and the fear outweighed the excitement and I suspended my attempts to contact Sparrow Records.

In the meantime, people in my community encouraged me to make a recording of predominantly Catholic music. I began to receive thousands of dollars from various people and ended up going back to Alexandria to record at what is now called Gaither Studios. I made another full-length recording of Catholic music called *Come to His Love*. God is still using this recording.

As I think back, this is where Satan began to insidiously invade my thoughts with equal portions of fear of success and fear of failure. I certainly couldn't see it at the time. It was as though a veil crept into my spiritual vision. And why wouldn't Satan go to work on me at a time like that, when I was at a potential crossroads and at the height of my music ministry? I know fear is not of God, and that's where the Enemy got his foot in the door and began to work. He did not want that door to open to me. He gets in wherever he can and pecks away little by little in ways that are rarely obvious.

Little did I know my landscape was about to change again. My new CD was a success. God blessed the music in spite of me. Yet, I secretly began to be tempted in a variety of ways and was eventually drawn back into a lifestyle similar to that of many years ago. The battle began, and Satan had his way with me. Temptation, guilt, shame, and secrecy. As I relive this by writing about it, I wonder how could I have been so deceived? It grieves me so. It grieves me so.

At the same time, the sexual abuse scandal broke out about the priests, and that fueled my rebellion even more. I felt deceived by the church somehow. After all, I had chosen the Catholic Church as an adult, and to find out this had been going on for years, threw me into a fury. I was unconsciously looking for anything to justify my choices. The real deception was going on in my heart, but I was so blinded I couldn't see it.

۴

I can say now, after coming back, that no matter what the priests did, Jesus is still Jesus. He died for our sins and He instituted Eucharist. This is our church; this is our faith.

۴

This downward spiral drew me into a life of spiritual rebellion. I stopped singing and eventually left the Catholic Church. That's exactly what Satan wanted. For ten years I was a prodigal, wandering and squandering. How could this have happened? I knew better. My spiritual landscape went from the mountaintops to a slimy pit; it was no longer pretty. The Devil won.

Thankfully, my wandering never took me beyond the Lord's reach. Trying to find my way back, I went to the Methodist church for a time. It wasn't a bad place, but it just wasn't the right fit for me. Then I wandered to Unity for a while, and that wasn't the right fit, either. So I decided it might feel right if I went back to my roots in the United Church of Christ. That didn't last long, since it proved not to be the place for me, either. Although I was able to sing in all those places, I felt like a wandering minstrel with no place that felt like home.

Throughout those years, I did meet a lot of wonderful people in all those places. But it just wasn't where I was supposed to be. I was called to be Catholic, and nothing else would feel right until I came home.

۴

Have you ever wandered off the path? Maybe you never left your church, but perhaps you've wandered away in your heart. Maybe you've become lukewarm in your faith. Maybe you've allowed other things to get in the way of your walk. God longs for our coming home to Him to live deeply, a new life and a new path. Where are you at in your faith journey? He loves. He waits. Come home in a deeper way.

Wandering in the Wilderness of Life

Wilderness Wandering

۴

*Long have you waited for me, Jesus, to
come back to you with all my heart.*

*How grateful I am that my wilderness wandering
never took me beyond your reach.*

*Like the sun that burns off the morning fog, let your grace
continue to burn off the layers of ego that dull my senses
and limit me from experiencing fully the joy of your love.*

*I'm trusting that I am right where I should be on my path
back. God, make my wandering count for something.*

~Cindy Staton~

The Journey Home

·Chapter 6·

The Journey Home

The Path that Led Me Home

۴

Coming back to the Catholic Church was a long road. I need to back way up so you can see how God mapped out my journey home.

۴

After sixteen years of owning my own business and opting not to accept the embroidery management position I decided to liquidate and get a regular job with some benefits. I got a factory job that paid well, and I was grateful for it. I thought I had it made and would work there till I retired.

Well, that was not to be. In under two years, my job was sent to Mexico, and I was laid off. I had no college degree, and I had sold all my sewing machines. I was at a total loss as to what to do. I was sort of angry at God. Remnants of my rebellion were still with me.

A program under the North American Free Trade Agreement (NAFTA) was retraining people to become more employable. I took a computer training program and hated every minute of it. But I didn't know what else to do.

Eventually I stumbled across the book *I Could Do Anything if I Only Knew What It Was, by Barbara Sher*. It asked two questions: What would your job from hell be and what would your job from heaven be? I knew immediately that a job from hell for me would be working at a computer all day.

As far as a job from heaven, I didn't know, but I knew it would be working with people instead of computers. One day a friend came over very stressed and asked if I would pray with her. I was happy to do that. I noticed how tired she was and suggested she lay back and relax for a bit. While she rested, I went to the kitchen to do dishes. Then suddenly, I had an aha moment. The Lord showed me that helping people to find peace and comfort was my calling. My next thought was massage therapy. I got out the phone book, closed my eyes, and it opened up to Carlson College for Massage.

I called to find out more about it and made an appointment to visit. When I arrived, I was able to speak to the owner. She was impressed with my excitement but informed me classes had started two weeks prior. I was bold enough to ask if there was any way she would let me start late if I made up all my time. She said she'd never allowed that before, but because I seemed so sure of myself, she said yes.

I quit the computer school and was in massage school the next day. My first day of class was their first day of hands-on training. The instructor observed me and asked if I had done this work before? I said "no." She remarked, "You're a natural. Your touch looks like that of someone who has been doing this for years."

It felt right to me. It felt like ministry in body, mind, and spirit. I graduated near the top of my class, got my degree, and started my own private practice, Safe Harbor Massage. About two and a half years into my practice, I began to wonder if this was all there was. My sense was no, but I didn't know what the *more* was. One day I stumbled across an article in one of my massage therapy magazines about hospice massage. That was it! That was the more.

I immediately had a burning desire to do that. I contacted the article's author, and he gave me the name of an instructor. I flew to Vermont to take a class on cancer massage. Three days after I got back, I sensed the Lord letting me know it was the day to call Hospice of Mercy, a Catholic hospice. I was immediately connected to the director. I introduced myself to her and told her I felt I was being called to this work. She said, "My goodness, I can feel the excitement coming through the phone lines from you."

I said, "I can't tell you how strongly I feel I'm supposed to be doing this work."

"Well, I have to tell you, it's interesting that you called today. I am sitting at my desk right now, writing a job description.

For the first time ever we have decided to hire a massage therapist."

I went for a personal interview and was hired half time. Eventually I gave up my private practice and went full time. That was nearly ten years ago. It's not a job; it's a calling that I'm honored to do. Providing comfort and peace to those nearing the end of this life's journey is humbling. I'm able to incorporate singing to my patients at times during the massage as well. My hands massage the body, and I pray my voice massages the soul.

You may be wondering what this story has to do with coming back to the church. Many of my patients have been Catholic and appreciate Catholic music, especially the "Ave Maria." I often sing Ave Maria during the massage. Some of them knew me from years of singing in concerts and had no idea I'd left the church.

Mary was drawing me in so gently once again, using all of these opportunities to bring me back. I was asked to sing at many funerals. One of my patients had been to Medjugorje, so we had an immediate connection. She told me she had been praying to find someone to sing "Ave Maria" at her funeral. No coincidence; God incidence.

These kinds of things continued to happen over time, and my heart softened. The longing to receive Jesus in Eucharist was coming back. The prodigal wanted to come home. One weekend I finally decided to go to Mass. I went to a church I'd never attended, and as only God could have orchestrated, Lorrenne was there. (She was the one who sponsored me into the church.) She was not a member of this church, either. We hadn't seen or spoken to each other for a long time. She was sitting there, praying the rosary, when I walked up and sat down next to her. Her reaction was one of surprise and joy, much like the father in the prodigal son story. She welcomed me. I have to believe the Blessed Mother was overjoyed as well, because while we were sitting there, we both witnessed the miracle of the sun, pulsating and spinning through one of the skylights in the church ceiling. As Lorrenne continued to pray her rosary, she looked down, and it had turned gold. It was as if the Blessed Mother was smiling down on this event.

The next week was Holy Week. I made a call to go to reconciliation and was able to be back home for Easter. "I was lost, and now I'm found. Was blind, and now I see." Praise God!

Part Two

Landscapes of a Sacred Journey

Babi

·*Chapter 7*·

Babi

۴

When I was a teenager, I did some volunteer work for the Council on Aging. I've always had a heart for the elderly. I was part of what they called the friendly visitor program. I visited an old Czech lady every week for several years. After my official visits for the council came to an end, my relationship with her did not.

I called her Babi, which means grandma in Czech. We became very close, and she felt like a grandma to me. In fact, when I got married, I had her ushered into the church as one of my grandparents. She called me her angel. We bonded immediately when through one of our first conversations, we discovered her son had been in my grandfather's Boy Scout troop with my dad. She thought God brought me to her. I think it was a mutual match made in heaven for both of us.

Babi was a widow, and her only son died in World War II. She was very much alone (or so I thought) except for one niece on her deceased husband's side who occasionally checked in on her. Babi and I went to the parks for picnics, to the zoo occasionally, and to the grocery store. Mostly I was there to provide companionship.

She lived very frugally. When I met her she still used a Sears and Roebucks fold-up canvas bathtub for bathing and a woodburning cookstove in her kitchen. While she was hesitant to accept any assistance from the Council on Aging, her social worker and I were able to convince her to at least let them put in a new bathtub and toilet for her. But she wouldn't hear of getting rid of her woodburning stove. Babi was a very proud lady, and it was difficult for her to allow anyone to do for her.

۴

Babi was Catholic and had a strong devotion to Mary. Her rosaries hung on the floor lamp next to her bed. I don't recall ever talking to her about them; I just remember being drawn to them.

۴

As the years went by, Babi and I grew much closer. She trusted me more than anyone in her world. As far as I knew, there was just her niece, and she didn't seem to make herself known too much. Babi began to talk to me about her will and her wishes. I thought maybe I would one day be the one to handle things when she passed, although nothing was legally done that would have allowed me to do so. She always said she wanted to change her will and include me in it, but it never happened. I'm glad it didn't, as I was there only for her and not for personal gain. She told me where she kept her will. She had it all wrapped up in cellophane and rubber bands, which she seemed to do with all her important papers and bank books. Whenever I saw anything wrapped that way, I knew it must be important to her.

As I mentioned earlier, she lived very frugally, and everything she had was old. It wasn't that she was a collector of antiques, but most of what she had was antique because she never bought anything new.

۴

Babi's health began to fail. She started having episodes of excruciating, unbearable pain in her face. She called me in the middle of the night on several occasions, needing me to come over to be with her. Things continued to change with her, and one day I received a call from her niece, saying Babi was in the hospital. She was found wandering outside, partially clothed and very confused. The police contacted her niece. She was admitted into the psych ward.

I went to see her immediately. When I saw her, her eyes and skin were very jaundiced. I told them she needed to be on a medical floor for further testing. It turned out she had advanced stages of pancreatic cancer. According to the doctor, Babi had only a couple weeks to live.

Babi was confused and began to lose her English, reverting to her native language. I constantly reminded her to speak

English. She was upset and convinced one of the nurses had stolen her savings book from her purse. She insisted that I go to the bank and put a lock out on the account.

She asked me to bring her rosary to her. Two rosaries hung on her lampstand, and I took both of them. When I got back to the hospital, I asked her if I could have one of them. She said yes. At the time, I knew nothing about how to pray the rosary, but I was drawn to it. How fitting that when she passed, the rosary was the only thing I received, and she gave it to me personally. Just as it should have been.

۴

Prior to her death, I was writing about my relationship with Babi. As I wrote, I paused and wondered if it was to be her eulogy. As it turned out, it was. I read what I had written at her funeral as well as sing "Ave Maria." There was not a dry eye.

I was amazed to find out she had family who lived in other states. Sad that they came out of the woodwork after she died.

When the niece called me about her passing, she asked if I wanted to go to the funeral home with her and help plan Babi's service. I was very happy to do that. The funeral director asked if anyone was able to stay in the house overnight for a few days, as there are people who watch the obituaries and break into houses during those times. I told the niece my husband and I would be glad to do that, as she had small twin boys that would have made it difficult for her.

My husband, Dave, and I packed a few things and went to Babi's house. The first night we talked about stories of people who were thought to be very poor, but on their deaths, find out they had money. Well, call it the Nancy Drew in me, I was curious. Years prior to her death Babi had taken me upstairs to show me her son's room. She had left it exactly as it was when he left for the service. There was another bedroom up there, but since I had known Babi, she never used it to sleep in. It was storage.

As our curiosity grew, Dave and I decided to venture upstairs and do some looking. Much to our surprise there were a lot of important things wrapped in cellophane and rubber bands. One of the first things I found was a bank savings book. I immediately wondered if she hid it up there for safekeeping and forgotten it. That could be why she thought someone had stolen it in the hospital.

The search continued; we found cash—a lot of cash. Some was hidden in cases of toilet paper. (You could tell she had lived through the Depression because she had stocked up on a lot of toilet paper, paper towels, and so on.) She had rolls of quarters wrapped in cellophane in a metal navy box in her son's closet. She had money stashed in coat pockets and many other places. When we stopped looking, we'd found $6,000.

Dave and I were living under hard times when this all happened. We ate a steady diet of eggs, soup, and rice. He had lost his job, and I had just started my sewing business. Things were not easy. As the money continued to pile up,

Dave said, "You know, she would have wanted you to have this."

I said, "Satan is using you to get to me." As honest as I am, I have to admit my spiritual vision was clouded because I, too, believed Babi loved me more than anyone left in her world and probably would have wanted me to have it.

I thought about the bank book again and wondered if it was a duplicate of the one in her purse that, along with her will, was at our house for safekeeping. I wanted to go home to compare the two, but we didn't dare leave all that money in the house while we were gone. After all, we were staying there to guard against vandals. So we gathered all the money at 2:00 am and ventured across town. When we got home, I grabbed her purse. Just as we were leaving to go back, I grabbed my Bible and said, "I'm not going anywhere without this."

When we returned to Babi's house, it was very late; or shall I say early. Dave was exhausted and went to sleep. I told him I was not going to sleep until I got an answer from God on this. I closed my eyes and opened the Bible. It opened to 1st Peter, chapter 5. I'm going to quote the entire portion because it is so powerful.

> To the elders among you, I appeal as a fellow elder, a witness of Christ's sufferings and one who also will share in the glory to be revealed; Be shepherds of God's flock that is under your care, serving as overseers—not because you must but because you are willing, as God wants you to be *not greedy for money,*

but eager to serve: not lording it over those entrusted to you, but being examples to the flock. And when the chief Shepherd appears, you will receive the crown of glory that will never fade away. Young men, in the same way be submissive to those who are older. Clothe yourselves with humility toward one another, because God opposes the proud but gives grace to the humble.

Humble yourselves therefore, under God's mighty hand, that He may lift you up in due time. Cast all your anxiety on Him because He cares for you.

Be self-controlled and alert. Your enemy the devil prowls around like a roaring lion looking for someone to devour. Resist him standing firm in the faith, because you know that your brothers throughout the world are undergoing the same kind of sufferings.

And the God of all grace, who called you to His eternal glory in Christ, after you have suffered a little while, will himself restore you and make you strong, firm and steadfast. To Him be the power for ever and ever. Amen.

۴

The cloud was immediately lifted, and I knew the Enemy had been defeated. Truth be known, this may have all happened to keep the niece and other family members honest.

I called the niece the next day and told her what happened. She said, "Wow, I can't believe you're so honest." Looking back at the Scripture, she was my flock at that moment.

We went to the bank and deposited all the money in Babi's account. We placed a lot of the old coins in her safety deposit box, as she had some coins that were over a hundred years old.

۴

At the funeral, just before they closed the casket, the niece removed the crucifix from the lid of the casket and handed it to me, saying, "You should have this." I was happy to receive it, and it meant a lot.

The day after the funeral, I met her at the house to return the key. When she walked in she had a strange look on her face. I asked her what was wrong. She said, "I don't believe you. When I got home after the funeral, I heard a voice in my head say, *You sure fell for that hook, line, and sinker.* I think you knew the money was there all the time, and that's why you were so eager to stay in the house. I think there was probably more money, and you just gave some of it back to make it look good."

I was never so blindsided in my life. I told her God could strike me dead there and then, and I knew I would go to heaven with a clear conscience because I did the right thing. I knew Satan had gotten to her big time. When I left, I handed the crucifix back to her and said, "I think you need this more than I do." When I got home, I knelt at my bedside, crying out to God, knowing this was not my battle to fight. This was a battle of principalities.

How fitting the only thing I had in my possession from my whole relationship with Babi was her rosary.

A week later, I was listening to Christian radio, and they were having a contest to win a Christian album. The catch was that if you won, you had to send it to someone who you knew needed it. I'd never won anything before, but I decided to give it a try. And I won! Guess who I had it sent to? The niece, of course. I never saw or spoke to her again, although I did hear through the grapevine from one of Babi's friends that they had found another $4,000 in the house. I can only hope she came to believe in the truth.

As for me, I thank God I remained faithful at a time when finances were extremely hard. God remained faithful as well.

The following week I got a call from one of my subcontracted businesses about a large order of jackets that needed to be done as soon as possible. That gave me the chance to prove myself. My business took off, and within six months, we had to move to a larger house with a basement big enough for my business. I went from a one bedroom sewing room to a full basement operation with four industrial sewing machines and six employees. The work never stopped coming. I ran that business for sixteen years.

God is so good.

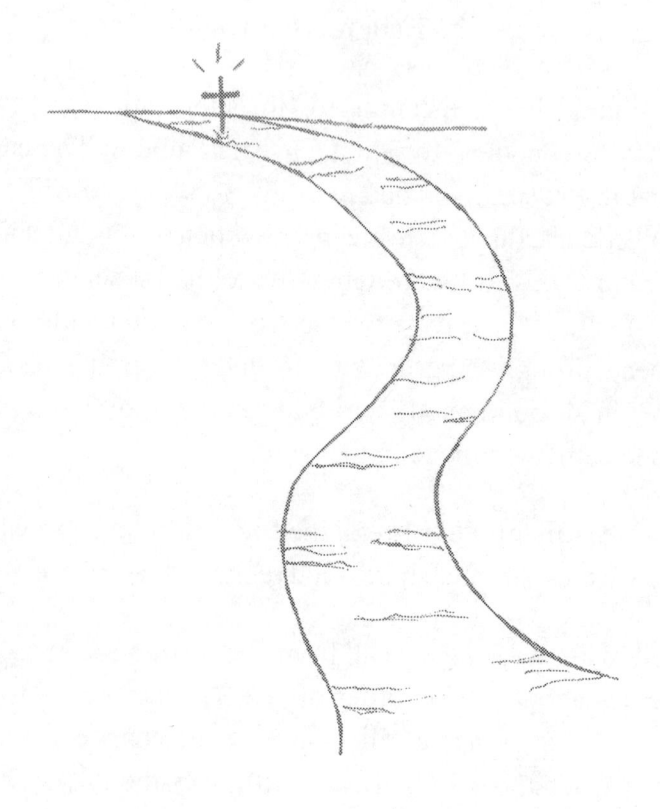

Landscapes of a Sacred Journey

Be Still And Know

That I Am God
(Psalm 40 v 10)

·Chapter 8·

Be Still and Know that I Am God

(Psalm 46:10)

۴

It was a hot, sultry week in July when I chose to take a week of silence. I went to a beautiful retreat called Christ in the Wilderness in Stockton, Illinois. Getting there was quite the adventure. I was supposed to call Sister Julia when I got close, so she could meet me at the end of the lane and guide me in. I didn't realize my cell phone plan didn't include this out-of-range area. To make matters worse, I was lost. I happened to see a little old lady working in her yard, so I stopped by and asked for directions. "Excuse me, but I'm looking for Christ in the Wilderness." I didn't realize till later how strange that must have sounded. I chuckled when I could understand her hesitant response. She did, however, let me use her phone. I was grateful I hadn't stopped at a gas station for directions; they might have thought I was out of my mind.

Anyway, I finally arrived. There were three hermitages on the land, all secluded from each other. There was also a small gazebo chapel and eighty acres of beautiful, lush forest with miles of walking paths conducive to reflection and meditation.

When I first arrived, I drove in long enough to unload my car. From that point on, everything was on foot. I couldn't help but notice there were a lot of butterflies around. Butterflies are about transformation, new life, and becoming. I wondered if this was to be a theme for my stay. I spent the rest of the afternoon getting settled and unpacked. I went to bed early as I wanted to start my first full day when everything was waking up.

I decided to start my day in the chapel. As I left my little hermitage and walked downhill toward the chapel, I noticed a pure white butterfly flying around my head. It gracefully flew around me as if to get my attention. I instinctively decided to follow it. It flew directly to a tree stump just outside the chapel door. A butterfly was carved on a plaque attached to the stump. Along with the butterfly was the Scripture, "Be Still and Know that I Am God." That was the Lord letting me know He was with me. What a wonderful way to start my five days of silence.

I went inside the gazebo chapel to spend time before the Lord in the tabernacle. I went there to be with Him and to be with me, willingly opening my heart and mind to see and hear Him within and around me. I asked that He walk with me.

۴

Coming to the silence is challenging at first. In the first few hours, I was aware of feeling anxious. I longed for the quiet, yet there is a natural unwinding of life that occurs on the path toward silence. The journey from the external to the internal is about letting go of all that keeps the mind engaged in chatter. Like going into the depth of the ocean beneath the current. Deep into the silence where the Savior and the soul come together.

۴

As I left the chapel to begin my first walk into the woods up a very steep hill. The parallels of life's journey and little lessons began immediately. I could not make this climb in a hurry. Lesson #1: Walk slow and steady; don't look to the goal or place of arrival, or you'll miss the beauty of what you see right where you are. As I continued to walk, there were places along the path to sit and rest. Lesson #2: Take time often to be quiet, to rest, to be aware, to find peace.

As I continued, I came to a place where I could choose different paths. I had no idea where any of them led or how I would find my way back. Lesson #3: Trust that whatever path you prayerfully choose in the wilderness of life, it will take you where you're supposed to be—even though there may not be signposts along the way. The Lord is guiding. Trust.

As the day came to a close, this theme of transformation continued to become evident. While I sat on the deck at my hermitage, a butterfly landed on my leg. As I moved, it flitted about. I held out my hand, and it landed on it. It was more than just a landing pad. We shared minutes together. Was this the Lord again coming to let me know He is still with me? I wondered, *Who's holding who? What am I to learn from this?* I decided to do some drawing and what came to mind was a cocoon opening and a butterfly emerging from it. As I finished the drawing the thought came, *Broken open to Become.*

Many pondering questions came to me. Is there something broken that keeps me from becoming? Is it in my brokenness that I become? Where am I at in this stage of metamorphous? Have I emerged from a cocoon about to take flight to a new experience? New heights?

As I continued to draw, I began to hear that still small voice, so I immediately put my drawing down and started writing what I heard. The following is what I heard.

۴

> My child, I am speaking to you through butterfly because she has a similar evolution as you. I inspired you with words to a song a few years ago. "Set Me Free to Be." I remind you of this now because your prayer in that song is now being answered.

Line by line, some of the lyrics of the song were explained to me.

"What holds me back from being who I want to be?"

Answer: "It was not yet your time; as with the butterfly, you have now done the necessary struggling to make you strong enough for your flight."

"The one who holds the gifts, the one who holds the key."

Answer: "You do hold the gifts, I gave them to you. You have had them always. You have talents as well, but your true gift is who you are."

"Mere glimpses of what's deep within me, is it courage that I lack? The future seems so frightening, but there's no turning back."

Answer: "This is true. I have given you snapshots of how you can touch humanity, but you were still in your cocoon. Your cocoon is beginning to break open for you to spread your wings and show your real beauty. Your wings are your heart."

"I long to let go what's inside of me, what's been in captivity. Set me free."

Answer: "You are being set free to be who you were designed to be. You can do no other. Spread your heart wings and fly, dear one, and like the butterfly, touch hearts with gentleness and grace. This is the right time for you and for those who I bring. Your cocoon has been a place of safety, but it has also held you captive to your old stories and false beliefs. You are now strong enough to let them fall away and allow your true self to emerge. I am with you always."

۴

These days of silence were truly transformative. I had watched the dance of the butterflies, listened to the symphonies of the birds, and the wind move through the trees. I saw a masterpiece of beauty that no artist could ever truly capture. I heard the silence … and felt God's profound presence. Amen is all I can say. Amen.

Anything you do for the least of my brothers, you do unto me.

(Matthew 25 v 40)

·Chapter 9·

The Can Man

۴

It was a time in my life when money was very tight. I had gone through my divorce, and things were very difficult. In an effort to supplement my income I began rummaging through trash cans in car washes and other places of public refuse to find pop and beer cans for cash. I wasn't destitute, but can cash did help.

One night after dark, I decided to take my cans to the store and turn them in to get a few groceries. When I arrived, an old man was rummaging through the trash outside the store. Part of me wished I had gotten there sooner. As I got closer to the door, I heard that still small voice in my heart say, *Give him your cans.* I knew the Lord was speaking.

I immediately began to bargain with God about this. *What if this man is a wino, Lord? I don't want to contribute to his habit. Tell ya what I'll do; I'll turn my cans in and follow him to see if he buys alcohol.*

What I was about to witness was quite the contrary. This man had to weigh a potato and a chunk of cheese to make sure he had enough money. I continued to watch, and when I saw him looking for the smallest jar of peanut butter he could get, I knew I had to act. The Holy Spirit was prompting me strongly; my heart was pounding out of my chest. I knew it was time to move and move <u>now</u>!

With compassion for this man, I approached and said, "Sir, you don't know me, but I couldn't help but notice that you are struggling. I don't have much, but what I have I'm glad to share with you." I had $6.00, so I gave it to him. His eyes opened wide with surprise and gratitude. You would have thought I had given him much more. He told me he'd been living in a boxcar, was discovered, and had to leave. All he had were his bicycle and his cans. He thanked me, and that was the end of it. Or so I thought.

I had a peace knowing I'd done the right thing. But the miracle is I never saw the man leave the store and never saw his bike. It was as though he had disappeared. When the realization came to me that he just seemed to have vanished, I again heard the Lord say, "Anything you do for the least of my brothers, you do unto me." (Matthew 25:40).

Oh my God, could it be that I was visited by an angel of the Lord? If this were a test, I think I passed. I never intended to share this story. It was a moment of surrender and obedience not to be bragged about. What came next made this whole story one that screams of God's faithfulness if we just trust Him.

Three days later, I was to take a walk with a friend and drove to her home to pick her up. When she got in the car she noticed some money tucked nicely next to the recline lever between the seats. She picked it up and handed it to me, asking if it was mine. I told her no, yet I knew no one else had been in my car. When she handed it to me, I noticed it was three $20 bills. Crisp and new—so new they were stuck together. When I held them in my hand, the Lord spoke once again. "It is ten times over the amount you gave." I was so grateful and humbled. I still am today as I write this. He is so faithful. I was able to buy groceries, but the greater food was that for my soul.

Part Three

Landscapes of a Sacred Journey

· Chapter 10 ·

Meditations and Musings on Life, Death, and Letting Go

۴

I have always been somewhat of a contemplative person. One who tries to see the deeper meaning of life. As I have wrestled with my own inner struggles, I have found that writing brings a peace to my soul that nothing else can do in quite the same way.

In recent years of working at Hospice, I have been with a lot of patients and families as they face the harsh reality that life will never be the same for them. The letting go of what is, and trying to prepare for what will be is not an easy path to be on. It has caused me to do a lot of reflection and soul searching about life, death, loss, surrender, acceptance and letting go.

The following section of the book is devoted to my inner reflections on those very things.

Once again, I invite you to ponder and pray.

There is Strength in Weakness

Chapter 11

Strength in Weakness

Jesus
Show me the softer way. In my weakness I'm asking
for your strength. Give me the grace and perseverance to
meet my addiction and all that drives it, with love.
Help me...
To see you in me and live through that lens
of empathy for myself and all others.
When I free myself from judgment, I am free
to see others through a softer lens as well.
I pray this in the name of the one who saves
me in my weakness, shelters me in the storms
of life and comforts me when I'm weary.
It is you Jesus, it is you...

~ Cindy Staton~

Bend with life rather than against

·Chapter 12·

IF

If I could let go as the trees let go
If I could only know what they know;
Fall is about releasing
that which has served me well for a time...
For a season.
If only I could be strong and well rooted
and yet bend with ease and grace,
If I could look at transition as seasonal and not harsh,
If the "IF" could become infinite faith,
ahh... there lies the wisdom of rest.

~ Cindy Staton

Rest In Me Dear One

·Chapter 13·

Rest in Me

Just be <u>with</u> me for now. Be still…
I am with you even now in your struggle.
I know dear one that you seek me and that you
have always been a seeker.
Just (Be) for now.
Rest in my security and calm from the clutter and
confusion in your mind.
Stay in your heart where (I AM)
and you will know peace.

Divine love does not struggle,
but rests….. Rest in Me…

~Cindy Staton~

Give Me New Vision in the Midst of the Mist and Mystery of this Life

Until I see you Face to Face

·Chapter 14·

Faith-filled Fog

As I observe the thick milky fog this morning I'm reminded that living on this side of the veil is much like walking through a fog. I can only imagine that on the other side of life in the everlasting, that there will be a clarity that is unlike anything we can see here. Everything will be understood and that which isn't understood won't matter, in the realm of <u>All</u> that does matter.

Creator God, master of all that is; even the fog; guide me through the fog of my life and give me a sense of sure footedness as I walk in faith.

Give me new vision in the midst of the mist and mystery of this life; to know that each step, each moment is guided by your loving presence until I see you clearly face to face.

Amen…..

~ Cindy Staton~

Loving Touch Can Change the World

·Chapter 15·

Hands

The simple touch of a hand can speak volumes to the human soul. I know of no other simple gesture that can elicit such a great response. Comfort, peace, compassion, reassurance, kindness, healing, and love.
Touch can change the world.

~Cindy Staton~

The answer to all of Life's problems and
Mysteries is not just in being connected to
The Divine Creator but in realizing too,
That we are at Onement with all......

Connected

DIVINELY INSPIRED DIVINELY NOURISHED DIVINELY GIVEN DIVINELY SERVING DIVINELY AT ONE

·Chapter 16·

Sacred Moments With Tree

۴

There's a tree at a nearby county park that I often spend quiet time and meditation with. I fittingly an simply call her "Tree". One day was different than any other. I have learned a lot about life as I have observed the cycle of its life from season to season. The parallels of Tree's life are much like mine. She has taught me that as the wind blows and the branches are tossed about, that I too must learn to bend with life rather against it. In the autumn she lets go of her leaves, as I too should try to let go of that which no longer serves me. This particular day as I was meditating, I heard a voice within me say, "Draw the tree". It took me by surprise; I never considered myself to be an artist and yet I felt compelled to respond to this request. I found an already used piece of paper in my car and began to sketch 'Tree'. After tree began to take shape on the page, I heard the voice again instructing me to "Draw yourself in Tree". I thought for a bit, wondering how I was to do this? As I continued my doodling, a person began to emerge from tree and I began to understand that this was a lesson for me. I continued to draw and listen. When I completed that step the voice came once again giving me divinely inspired words to be placed at the roots of Tree. Gods love is deeply planted within the soil of our soul so it is fitting then that we are Divinely Inspired, Divinely Nourished, Divinely Given, Divinely Cherished, and Divinely At One. The last time I heard the voice, I received the caption that would sum up the lesson... That we are all divinely connected; and why wouldn't we be? when we all come from the same source. There is much to be learned from this sacred connection.

~Cindy Staton~

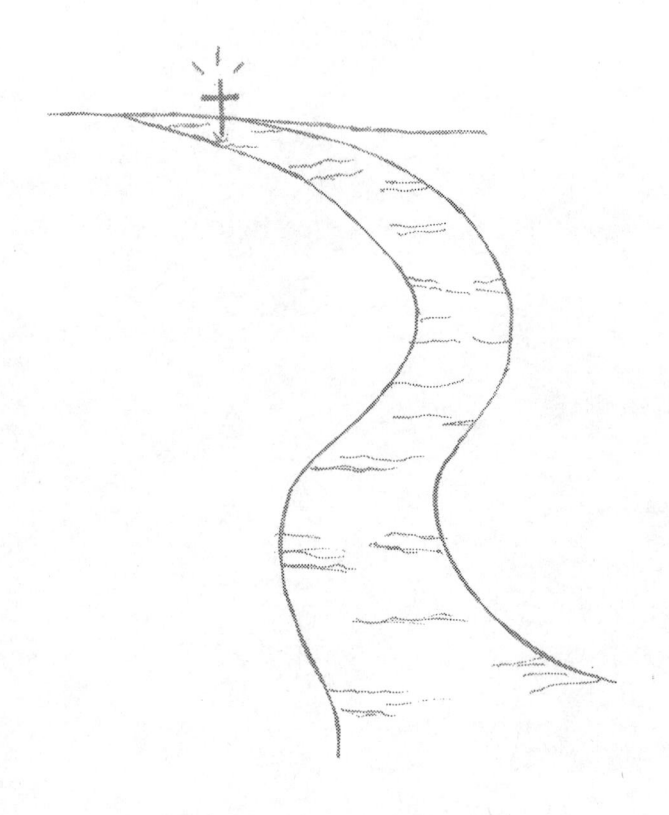

Landscapes of a Sacred Journey

Spiritual Growth Happens in the Silence

·Chapter 17·

Growth in the Silence

*Spiritual growth is somewhat like that of a flower;
it grows in the silence.
If you watched it all day long you wouldn't see
the transformation from a bud to a
blossom, and yet change happens.
Spiritual growth is much the same;
I'm not always
aware of the change and yet over time,
reflection of what was is no longer.
Change has occurred, growth has happened, but when?
Everything and I are continually becoming
in the dawn of mysteries
unknown and the impermanence of each day that
comes and goes............*

~Cindy Staton~

We must die to our old ways of being to become.

·Chapter 18·

New Life

۴

*Whenever new life comes, it's because what was
is no longer. As with a chrysalis it must die to its
existence in the cocoon before it can become. The time
in the cocoon however is vital to its strength in being
able to break out of its old existence and fly.
When is the perfect time? We will never understand the
mystery of perfect timing but we must trust that we have
been for a very long time gaining strength enough to break
out of our old existence so we can fly toward new life.
Once we fly there is no going back, no more
than a butterfly can fly back to its cocoon.
God help me to break through the shell of my
cocoon; let all that holds me too securely to myself
fall away, so that I may fly, trusting that you are
guiding my flight and know where I am to land.*

~ Cindy Staton

Letting Go creates room for the New to Come.

·Chapter 19·

Release and Reshape

Letting go does not mean forgetting what has happened or forgetting who may have wronged you; but rather it's in the letting go of the power it has to continue hurting you and holding you captive. Letting go allows room for the gift of realizing the life lessons that can be learned from each wound. We are who we are and pain can shape us into whoever we choose to become....

~ Cindy Staton ~

*Faith is allowing the Mystery of
God to be just that...*

A Mystery

Chapter 20

Let God Be God

*Let God Be God
and let go of that which no
longer serves you.....
When we don't understand the
mysteries of life, we must stand
within the mystery and allow
it to move in and through us.
Wisdom comes from allowing
God to be God in the midst
of our questioning.*

~ Cindy Staton~

Threshold to New Life

·Chapter 21·

Is There Death?

There is Life, but is there really Death? or is it just a moment in time that is nothing more than a threshold to new life? We come into being into flesh and along the way we have many "deaths" or moments of transition when we let go of one way of being, doing...living. Those moments in time when like it or not, life changes and we are forever changed as a result of it. We willingly or unwillingly surrender, let go, become, which is rebirth, not death.

When we leave this earth, is it death that happens? I think not; it is also rebirth. A return to where we came from.

As St. Theresa said, "It is not death that will come for me... it is God." It is not death, it is transition it is transformation.

Life is a miracle and if there is death it is its equal.

~ Cindy Staton

A Dead End

· Chapter 22 ·

A Dead End

It's difficult to articulate what I'm feeling these past few days other than loss. Saying good bye is so hard. Good bye brings with it finality; like a road that suddenly just comes to an end. A dead end..... The memories live on for sure, but the journey together is over and it leaves me with an emptiness that has no words. It's human nature that wants to fill whatever is empty but it is more fitting to sit with this empty and let it be what it needs to be; to feel the sadness, to feel the loss, to feel the emptiness....... to get to healing.

The mystery of life and death will forever continue to be mystery. Peace comes when I'm able to stand within the mystery and accept the reality that what I'm grasping for I will never reach until I too am on the other side.

~ Cindy Staton ~

Our legacies live on and on...

·Chapter 23·

Legacies

What can we say about the mystery of life and death? Is it merely that we are here one day and gone another? I think rather that life is a cycle that has a beginning and an end; however the impact of a life never ends. The spirit or energy which each life gives to another is eternal. So then in life or death we leave a legacy that has endless ramifications.

In death the legacies remain even though the body does not. Energy has left and that space is filled with emptiness. Our hearts have a void that nothing else can quite fill in the same way. The memory will live on but the energy of the life now gone, is just gone. So how do we fill that space? Or is it more fitting that we hold that heart space as sacred for the life that was there. Loss is loss and I think it just has to be that way. Everyone who has had a part of our hearts will <u>forever</u> hold that place...

It is forever sacred space that no thing or no one else can fill......

~Cindy Staton~

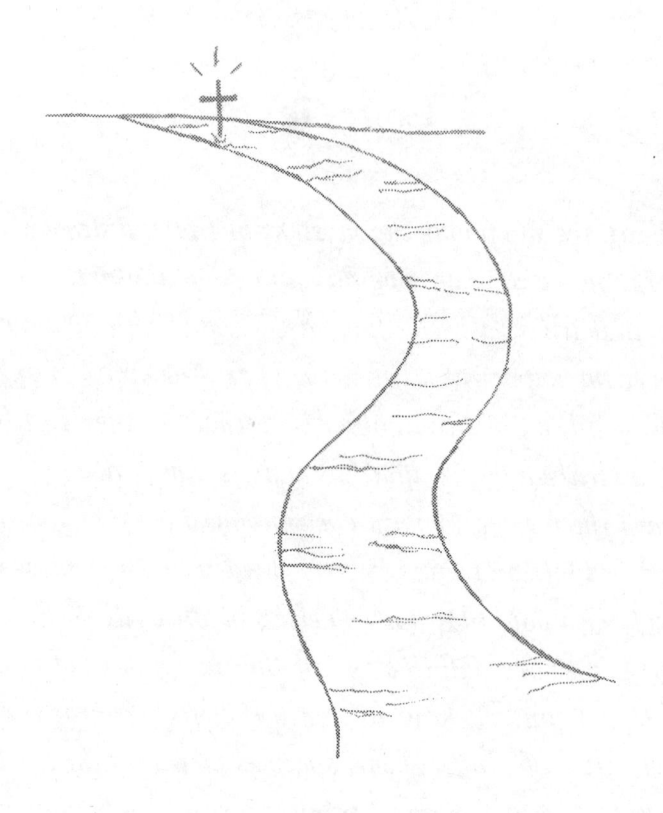

Landscapes of a Sacred Journey

Conclusion

۴

As you sit back and reflect on the stories I've shared, you can see that throughout my life, there has been a continual rise and fall between flesh and faith. My prayer is that with each fall; that I can continue to get up with a greater awareness of my need to walk even closer to my Savior. Do I have it all together? No way, but as one of the AA slogans states, it's about "spiritual progress rather than spiritual perfection."

In fact it is in the journey itself that we become that which He calls us to be. Sanctification and Surrender are synonymous in the pathway toward holiness.

۴

We all have a story and we all fall short of the glory of God. Thankfully, we have a God who can make all things new. He is much more interested in our future than in our past.

(Psalm 40 :1-3) "I waited patiently for the Lord; He turned to me and heard my cry. He lifted me out of the slimy pit, out of the mud and mire; he set my feet on a rock and gave me a firm place to stand. He put a new song in my mouth, a hymn of praise to our God."

This is my story, this is the Landscapes of a Sacred Journey

The journey continues.

God Bless you on your journey as well.

Closing Prayer

God,
You are the author and finisher of my faith and my life.
You are the one who chose me to manifest these stories through. I am humbled and grateful. I release this book back into your hands to do with it what You will.
You are truly the author.
Amen

Bibliography

۴

Scripture Quotes

Romans Chapter 8: 28 New International Version (NIV)

John Chapter 14: 6 New International Version (NIV)

Psalm 42: 1-2 New International Version (NIV)

Romans 3: 23 New International Version (NIV)

1st Peter 5: 1-11 New International Version (NIV)

Psalm 46: 10 New International Version (NIV)

Matthew 25: 40 New International Version (NIV)

Psalm 40: 1-3 New International Version
(NIV)

۴

Mathew Kelly's trademark slogan *
Best Version of Yourself

۴

Popular slogan from the Big Book in
Alcoholics Anonymous (AA)

"Spiritual Progress rather than Spiritual Perfection"

Credits
Author Photo by Sharon L. Svoboda

۴

My personal thanks to all who have been so much support throughout my life and particularly through this process.

You are all a part of this book because
you are all a part of my landscape.

May God Bless You All !

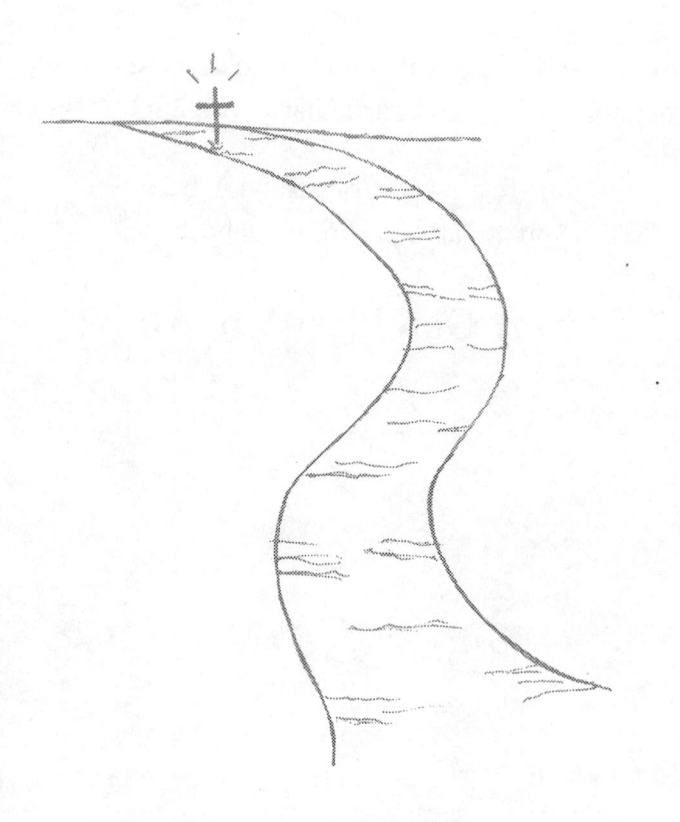

Landscapes of a Sacred Journey

Printed in the United States
By Bookmasters